Robinson Crusoe

DANIEL DEFOE

Level 2

Retold by Nancy Taylor
Series Editors: Andy Hopkins and Jocelyn Potter

Pearson Education Limited
Edinburgh Gate, Harlow,
Essex CM20 2JE, England
and Associated Companies throughout the world.

ISBN 0 582 426960

This edition first published 2000

NEW EDITION

3 5 7 9 10 8 6 4

Typeset by Pantek Arts Ltd, Maidstone, Kent
Set in 11/14pt Bembo
Printed in Denmark by Norhaven A/S, Viborg

Published by Pearson Education Limited in association with
Penguin Books Ltd, both companies being subsidiaries of Pearson Plc

Acknowledgements:
Photographs © BBC 1974

For a complete list of titles available in the Penguin Readers series please write to
your local Pearson Education office or contact: Penguin Readers Marketing
Department, Pearson Education, Edinburgh Gate, Harlow, Essex, CM20 2JE.

Contents

Introduction

The wind and rain were strong all night. The next morning I could not see the ship. It was under the sea, with my ten friends.

Robinson Crusoe is at sea when there is a great storm. His ship goes down, and everybody dies. Crusoe is on an island. But which island? Are there other people on the island? Will he have to stay there for a long time? Where will he live? What will he eat? What will he wear? This book tells Crusoe's exciting story.

Daniel Defoe, the writer of this book, was born in London in 1660. Defoe started to write when he was a young man. He wrote stories for newspapers and for the first magazines in England. In 1704 he started a magazine, *The Review*. It came out three times a week and there were stories in it about different places in Europe.

After some years, Daniel Defoe began to write books. His books were exciting and a lot of people enjoyed them. The idea for *Robinson Crusoe* (1719) came from the story of Alexander Selkirk. Selkirk went to sea in 1704. He fought with the captain of his ship, so the captain left him on the island of Juan Fernandez. Nobody lived on the island at that time. Selkirk stayed there from 1704 to 1709. Then an English ship came to the island and took Selkirk back to England.

Now, 300 years later, people all round the world know about the island lives of Robinson Crusoe and his man Friday from Daniel Defoe's great story.

Chapter 1   My Life at Sea

I go to sea

I was born in the year 1632, in York, a city in the north of England. I came from a good family, but I always wanted to go to sea. My father was from Germany. He came to York when he was a young man. My first name is Robinson, because that is my mother's family name. My father's last name was Kreutznaer, but English people can't say this. Now I am Robinson Crusoe.

My father was a clever man. He understood the world, and he loved me. He said, 'Stay in York. I will help you with money and a job. You can be happy here.' For a time I listened to my father, but the sea called to me.

One day in the city of Hull, on the north-east coast, I met a friend. We talked about his plans for the future. 'I'm going to sea on my father's ship', my friend said. 'Come with me. We will see the world!' This idea was wonderful to me. I forgot about my father and his kind words. I didn't say goodbye to him or to my mother. I went to the ship and began my new life. On that same day, 1st September 1651, we left Hull. The ship's journey was from Hull to London.

My first sea journey

On my first night at sea there was a heavy storm. I was afraid and I wanted to be at home in York. I wanted to forget about the sea. But there was no storm in the morning, so I forgot about home again.

But before the ship arrived at Yarmouth, there was a worse storm. We worked hard, but we couldn't bring the ship to land. I

1

left the ship in a small boat with the other men. We watched our ship. It went down to the bottom of the sea.

My friend's father said, 'Young man, go home. The sea is not the place for you.' I left my friend and his father and followed the road to London. I thought about my future. My first journey was bad, but I didn't want to go home. I looked for a ship. I wanted to go to sea again.

Journeys to new countries

I found a man with a ship. His next journey was to Guinea, on the west coast of Africa. He was a good man, and he helped me. I bought things in London and took them on the ship with me. Then I sold these things to the people of Guinea. I came back to England with £300 in my hand.

I used my money for a very long journey to Brazil. At the end of four years there, I had a large sugar farm. Life was good: I had money, a lot of land and no problems. But when I had no problems, I always found some! With other farmers, I planned a journey back to Guinea. We wanted tools and other things from Europe, and we wanted slaves for our farms from Africa. I got a ship ready for the journey.

I leave Brazil

On 1st September 1659, eight years after my first sea journey from Hull, I left Brazil for Africa. It was very hot and the weather was good. But after twelve days there was a great storm. The wind threw the ship this way and that way for nearly two weeks. There were eleven of us and we were afraid for our lives. Then early one morning, one of our men shouted, 'Land!'

The water came over the ship again and again. We didn't have much time. It was dangerous on the ship, so we put a small boat in the water. Then we got into it. But the sea and the wind were very strong, and we were very tired and weak. The wind turned the boat on one end and threw us into the sea.

I find land

The water played with me for a long time. It threw me on the land and pulled me back into the sea. Then it left me on the beach. I was very weak and ill. But I got up on my feet and ran to dry ground. Then I fell down again. My friends were dead, and I was nearly dead, too. That night I slept in a tree because I was afraid of the animals – and perhaps of the men in this strange place.

I go to the ship

When I woke, it was day. The sea was quiet, and the ship was about half a mile from the land. I had nothing with me – no food, no tools, no gun or knife. So I swam to the ship. I found many important things there: food and drink, guns, pens and paper, money, clothes, knives, books. I made a small boat and took these things to the land. I worked for three weeks and made eleven journeys between the beach and the ship. Then the storms started again, and I stayed on land.

The wind and rain were strong all night. The next morning I could not see the ship. It was under the sea, with my ten friends.

Chapter 2   The Island

I am on an island

Next I had to look round the country and find a place for my home. I took my gun and walked to higher ground. I was on an island. I could see the sea to the north, south, east and west. I could also see two small islands, about nine miles away to the west. I couldn't see any farms or people on my island. I saw a lot of birds, but I didn't know their names. On my way back I killed a great bird with my gun. At the sound of the gun, a lot of birds flew up and made loud noises in the sky.

I build a home

I found a good place for my home near the top of a hill. There was a large square of land with a small cave at the back. I had many things from the ship. From these I made a tent at the front of the cave.

Then I cut down young trees and built a strong wall round my home. The wall was nearly six feet high and eighty feet long. I worked on this wall for more than three months. I made the cave larger and put my things inside.

I finish the house

Now I had two rooms. I lived and slept in my tent. I used the cave for my food and water and for the things from the ship. It was also my kitchen and dining-room. There wasn't a door in my wall, but I could climb over it. I made some stairs, and each night I brought them into the cave. Then I could forget about animals and strange men. I could sleep easily.

After about ten or twelve days on the island, I thought of something. I wanted to remember the date. So I took down another tree, and I cut into it, in big letters:

I CAME TO THIS ISLAND ON 30 SEPTEMBER 1659

Each day I cut a small mark in the post. Every seventh mark was longer than the other marks. This showed the end of a week. A thicker mark, every thirty or thirty-one days, showed the end of a month.

I build things for my house

I wanted a table and a chair. These were the most important things for me. I wanted to sit at a table for my breakfast, lunch and dinner. I also wanted to write the story of my exciting and difficult life. Perhaps, one day in the future, I could show it to people.

Every job took a long time and a lot of hard work. I had to cut down trees with my tools from the ship. Then I made a good table and chair, some shelves and some boxes. I put the shelves on the walls of the cave and I put my things in boxes on the shelves. I was happy when everything was on a shelf.

Now I had a plan for my days. I walked out with my gun for two or three hours every morning. I usually found my food for the day in these hours. Then I worked in my house. I ate my lunch at midday. After lunch I slept for two hours because it was very hot. Then in the evening I worked again. At night I read and I began to write my story.

Chapter 3 I Look Round the Island

I find good fruit

After ten difficult months, I had a good home and a lot of food. Now I wanted to see the island. Was there anything in this country for me? There were no people on the island. But perhaps there were other interesting places and things.

On 15th July I went up the small river near my house. I found good land with trees and a lot of fruit. The weather was hot and the fruit was ready. It was very good, but I was careful. I ate only a little of the fruit on the first day. I remembered men on my ship from London to Guinea. They ate a lot of the strange fruits from Africa. Some men were very ill and two or three people died.

I thought of a good use for this fruit. I wanted to dry it in the sun and then have fruit every day. I couldn't carry a lot of fruit back to my house so I put it in the trees, very high above the ground. That night I climbed into a tree, too. I slept very well there. It was my first night away from my new home.

The garden

In the morning I walked and looked at the country round me. There was a lot of lovely green land and good water. It was a garden with many fruits and vegetables. It was a better place than the place near my house. I looked carefully at this beautiful land. I thought, 'I am the only person on this island, so this is my land!' Now I had a big job. I had to carry fruit and vegetables back to my house.

At home again, I thought, 'Is this the best place in my country for my house?' Only four miles away there was better land and a lot of fruit and vegetables. But here I was near the beach. I

After ten difficult months, I had a good home. . .

wanted to see a ship one day. I wanted to go back to England. So I stayed in my house near the beach and hoped for a ship.

Later I built a small tent near the 'garden'. This was my country house, and I went there often. I enjoyed the trees, and I ate the fruit and vegetables. In August I brought a lot of dry fruit back to my beach house.

The rain comes

There was rain every day for two months from the middle of August to the middle of October. The dry fruit was very good for me then. On some days I couldn't leave my house because the rain was very heavy. I couldn't always get food easily, but I had jobs inside my house at this time. I made plates, cups, spoons and many other things for my kitchen. I learned to make better food, too.

September the thirtieth was an unhappy day. One year on this island. One year without people or conversation. I looked at the marks on my tree: 365 days. I was very quiet and sad all day. Could I hope for anything in the future?

Chapter 4   My Country

I look at my country

After the rain stopped, I began to look round my country again. I walked past my country house and came to the west coast of the island. The sky was blue and I could see land to the west. I think it was about sixty miles from my island. Was it American land? Perhaps it was a dangerous place – perhaps cannibals lived there. In Brazil I heard many stories about cannibals. Many of them lived up and down this coast. I planned to stay on my island and forget about this other land. I had to wait for a ship from Europe. I had to be happier on my island.

On this journey round the island, I also found other animals and birds. I killed a number of the animals and carried the meat to my house. I was excited when I saw some parrots, too. I caught a young bird and took it to my house. After some years Pol, my parrot, could say my name.

On a later journey round the island I also caught a young goat. I brought the goat to my house, too. I wanted to have a lot of goats near my house, for their milk and their meat.

I make bread

I had a bag from the ship with old food for the chickens. I threw this dirty corn on the ground near my house because I wanted to use the bag. After some weeks new corn began to come out of the ground. Then I had a garden, too, and I could make bread. Everything was very hard work, but my life was better each day.

The months went past quickly, and then it was 30th September again. That year I wasn't afraid of the future. I was busy every day and interested in my house and my island. I read and thought. I remembered my father's kind words. I understood him now because I understood more about life. I could be happier on the island than I was in London or in Brazil.

Chapter 5   My Boats

I want a boat

Every day I thought about the islands to the west. A sea journey was dangerous, but it was perhaps the only way to leave my island. Perhaps those islands were the first stop on my journey back to England. Then I remembered the ship's boat. When the wind threw me and the other men into the sea, it also threw the boat on to the beach. This heavy boat was on the beach about one kilometre to the north of my house.

I made plans. I could use the boat for my journey to the islands. The boat was dry and good, but half of it was under the ground on the beach. I couldn't move it. This was a job for six or eight strong men. I worked for four weeks, but the boat didn't move. So I forgot this plan, but I didn't forget about the other islands or about England.

In the middle of my work on the boat, it was 30th September again. I had a quiet day and thought about my four years on this island. I enjoyed the good things in my life. I woke up every morning and planned my day. I worked with a smile on my face. I slept easily at night. I was happy.

New clothes

After four years here, I didn't have any food from the ship. And now my clothes were old and thin, too. I killed and ate a lot of animals, and I used the coats from these animals for my new clothes. First I made a very fine hat for my head. Then I made a jacket and short trousers. I was very dry in the rain because the animal hair was on the outside of my clothes.

I wanted an umbrella. I saw many people in Brazil with umbrellas because the sun is very hot there. My island was hotter than Brazil because the sun was stronger on 'my head. And an umbrella is good in the rain, too.

I worked for weeks on my umbrella. I made three before I was happy with one. But in the end I had a very nice umbrella. I put an animal coat on the outside of it. Then I could walk happily round the island in the rain and the sunshine.

*Then I could walk happily round the island in
the rain and the sunshine.*

I build a boat

After another five years I tried to make a small boat. I cut down a great tree. It was nearly six feet across at the bottom and five feet at the top. After the tree was on the ground, I cut out the centre of it with my tools. I worked on the inside and the outside of the boat for about six months. In the end I had a fine little boat. I put my gun, my umbrella, food and water into the boat and began my journey. I wanted to go round the coast of my island country.

But problems followed me and my boat. The sea was very dangerous on the east coast of the island. The wind was strong and I couldn't drive my little boat back to the beach. I fought the wind for hours and I was afraid. After many hours the sea was quiet again. I found the beach, but where was I? I went up the coast and found a small river. I left the boat there. I took my gun and my umbrella and began to walk. After three hours I found my little country house. I went inside and fell on my bed. I was very tired and ready for sleep.

Pol speaks to me

Hours later I heard a sound. 'Robin, Robin, Robin Crusoe. Sad Robin Crusoe. Where are you, Robin Crusoe?' I couldn't wake up, but I heard my name again. I was afraid for a minute. Then I opened my eyes and I saw Pol. He looked at me and spoke to me again. 'Robin Crusoe, where are you? Sad Robin Crusoe. Why are you here?' When I saw my parrot, I was very happy. I carried him home with me. I forgot about boats and ships again.

After eleven years on the island, I had more than fifty goats, a large garden, a farm with a lot of corn and two good houses. I made bread, cakes and butter. I had milk and dry fruit. I was busy every day. But then my life changed. Something wonderful happened!

Chapter 6   The Mark of a Man's Foot!

I am afraid

I was on the beach one day and found something different. It was the mark of a man's foot. I looked at this strange thing and I felt cold. How was this possible? I listened, and I looked round me. I could hear nothing. I could see nothing. I walked up and down the beach. Then I went to the mark again and looked at it. It was really there. Where did it come from?

I ran to my house. Every minute or two I stopped and looked behind me. Was there a man in the trees? Strange ideas ran through my head. Who was on *my* island? In *my* country?

I stayed inside my house for three days. I couldn't sleep. I felt afraid. What could I do? Were there people on the island? Did cannibals from other islands visit my island sometimes?

I make my house stronger

After three days I had a new idea. Perhaps the mark was from *my* foot. I went to the beach and put my foot on the mark. But my foot was smaller.

I went back home and made stronger walls round my house. I made seven small windows in my outside wall and put my big guns in them. I moved half of my goats to a different place. I put more trees round my two houses. Now nobody could see the two houses on the island. I worked on these jobs for more than two years. I did not see another mark on the beach!

I went back home and made stronger walls round my house.

Chapter 7   Cannibals!

I see a boat

One day, when I walked to the west coast of the island, I saw a boat on the sea. But was it really a boat? It wasn't near the island. When I came down from the hill, I couldn't see it. Perhaps the mark on the beach wasn't strange. Perhaps boats stopped at the island when there were storms at sea. Perhaps men from other islands came to my island for fruit or for goats.

Dead men's bones

I walked to a different place on the coast. On the beach, in the hot sun, I saw some bones. I looked at the bones carefully. They weren't from a bird or a goat or another animal. They were the bones of a man! So cannibals cooked and ate people here on my beach. Why did men do this to other men?

I watch for the cannibals

I felt ill, but I made my plans. First I moved my little boat and put it near my house. Then I found a place on top of a hill. From there I could watch the beach with the bones. I wanted to kill the cannibals when they came back with another man for their dinner.

I often thought about the cannibals. I couldn't work on my house and garden. Perhaps the cannibals could hear the noise of my tools. I was afraid, and I didn't want to meet them on the beach. I didn't often use my guns, and I was careful with fires. I found a bigger cave near my country house. I used this when I made a fire for bread and cakes or for meat. The smoke didn't leave this big cave.

I also moved some guns and other things to this bigger cave. I wanted to have guns near me when I was at my country house. I was more intelligent than 500 cannibals!

Every morning I took some guns and walked about three miles to my place on the hill. I watched and waited for the cannibals. But nobody came. Nothing happened. I watched every morning for months, but I didn't see anybody.

Then I went back to my old life and looked for food in the mornings. I didn't visit that hill for a long time. I tried to forget about the mark on the beach and the bones. I tried, but I couldn't forget.

I am afraid again

It was now the end of the summer of my twenty-third year on this island. I had a lot of work in my garden. I looked at the corn every morning very early. One morning, before it was light, I saw a fire on the beach. It was about two miles away, near the hill. I ran quickly to the hill and looked for the fire.

I saw nine men on the beach below me. They wore no clothes. They sat round a small fire. The weather was very hot, so the fire was for food. They danced – they moved their arms and legs quickly up and down. After an hour, the water in the sea was high on the beach. The nine men got into their boats and began to leave.

I ran back to my cave for my gun. When I came to the hill again, I saw their two boats on the sea. Then I saw three other boats. The five boats went north.

I went down to the beach. There were new bones – the bones of two men! I was very angry. Again, I wanted to kill them when they came back to the island. But they didn't often come to my island. I knew that now.

A ship arrives

For fifteen or sixteen months after the cannibals' visit to my island, I didn't sleep well. I woke up in the middle of the night and looked for men outside my walls.

On 16th May there was a great storm. The wind was very strong, and I couldn't sleep. Then I heard a sudden noise. I jumped and ran to my wall. Was it the sound of a gun at sea?

I went to the hill. I watched and listened. I heard more loud noises from the sea. Was there a ship near the island? Was there an accident? I couldn't help the ship, but perhaps the ship could help me.

I built a large fire on my hill. When my fire was big, it gave a lot of light. I heard the guns from the ship again. I had a fire on the hill all night. In the morning the weather was bad and I couldn't see very well. Where was the ship?

When the sky was blue again, I saw the ship. It was near the beach, but it was under the water. And where were the men from the ship? Were they on the great sea or at the bottom of it? I cried because there was nobody from that ship on the beach. Why didn't one man arrive on my island and speak to me? That was my saddest day in twenty-three years.

I go to the ship

I went back to my house and got ready for a journey to the ship. Perhaps there was a man on the ship. Perhaps he was ill and couldn't shout for help. I took bread and water, dry fruit, corn, milk and my gun. The journey was two hours in my boat.

On the ship I found eight dead men. There was no life there. The food was wet, but I found some bottles of wine, some good guns and some money. I also found some tools, some things for my kitchen and some fine shirts. I really wanted some shoes, so I took them from the dead men. They weren't English shoes but I was happy with them. I put everything into my boat and went home. I was very tired and sad at the end of that day.

I want to go home

I followed my plan every day, but I often looked at the sea. I thought about England. I wanted other ships to come near my island. I wanted to leave.

Sometimes I had strange ideas in my head. I had a friend on the island. We built a boat and found the way to England. This wasn't possible, of course, but I thought of a different plan.

When the cannibals came back to the island with other men for their dinner, I could kill the cannibals. I wanted to be friends with the other men, their prisoners.

Chapter 8   The Cannibals Come Again

Five boats

For two or three years, I watched again for the cannibals, but I didn't see them on my island. Then one morning I was on a hill and I looked down at the beach below me. I saw five boats on the beach, quite near my house. There were no men with the boats, but there were usually four or six men in each boat. So there were perhaps twenty or thirty men on the island. I went back to my house and cleaned my guns. Then I closed my house and went to the top of the hill again. I saw the cannibals.

From the hill I could see about thirty men on the beach. They had a big fire and there was meat on the fire. What animal did this meat come from? Some men cooked it. The other men danced round the fire.

Then the cannibals pulled two other men from a boat. They were prisoners. Were they more meat for the cannibals' dinner? One cannibal hit the shorter prisoner with a heavy tool. The prisoner fell. I think that he died very quickly. Two other cannibals cut into the dead man's stomach. Then they cut off his arms and legs.

A prisoner runs away

The other prisoner stood behind the dead man. The cannibals were busy and didn't look at him. In that minute, the prisoner looked round him, and then he ran as fast as possible across the beach. He couldn't see me but he came nearer and nearer to me and to my house.

The cannibals followed the prisoner, and I was afraid. But I didn't move – I watched the prisoner. After a minute or two, only three cannibals followed the prisoner. I felt happier now because the prisoner was a very fast runner. He was faster than the three cannibals.

There was a little river between these men and me. The prisoner stopped at this river and looked up and down. But when the cannibals were near, he jumped into the river. Then he swam across it. The river was fast and strong, but the prisoner could swim very well.

The three cannibals came to the river and stopped, too. One man couldn't swim. He left and went back to the beach.

I kill two cannibals

The other two men jumped into the water and swam slowly across the river. They weren't good swimmers. I had an idea in my head now. I thought, 'Can this prisoner be my friend?' I took my gun and ran quickly down the hill.

I was between the prisoner and the two cannibals. I shouted at the prisoner: 'Come here!' Then I ran to the first cannibal and hit him hard. I didn't use my gun because I didn't want the other cannibals to hear the noise. But the other man ran at me very fast. I had to use my gun. In a minute, the second cannibal was dead.

The prisoner was afraid of the noise from my gun. He looked at me and didn't move. I spoke quietly to him – I wanted to be his friend. He came near me, but he was very careful. He didn't know – was he my prisoner now?

Chapter 9   Friday

The prisoner

I looked at my 'prisoner'. He was a tall young man with strong arms and legs. He was about twenty-six years old, I thought. He had a good, kind face and intelligent eyes. His hair was long and black, but he had no hair on his face. He had a small nose and beautiful white teeth. He wore no clothes.

I spoke to him again and he came nearer. When he stood in front of me, I smiled. He fell on the ground and put my foot on his head. He wanted to be my slave. I pulled him to his feet and smiled at him again.

Two dead cannibals

But now we had a difficult job. One of the cannibals wasn't dead. He sat up and looked at us. The prisoner, or my slave, spoke to me. I didn't understand his words, but the sound made me very happy. After twenty-five years, somebody spoke to me!

My slave wanted my knife, so I gave it to him. He walked to the cannibal and cut off his head as quickly as possible. When the cannibal was dead, my slave laughed. He gave me the knife and the cannibal's head. Then he looked carefully at the other dead cannibal. He didn't understand about guns. How did the gun kill this man? I spoke to him, and he looked at me for a minute. Then he quickly put the two dead men under the ground. The other cannibals couldn't find them now.

My life with Friday begins

We walked to the big cave near my country house. My slave was very tired and hungry. I gave him bread, dry fruit and water. Then I made a bed for him and he slept for a short time.

When he woke up, my slave came out of the cave to me. Again he fell on the ground and put my foot on his head. I understood him and smiled at him. Then I began to speak to him. I said the names of many things in English. He said the words after me. Then I said, 'Your new name is "Friday", because today is Friday. We will remember this day with your name.' I also taught him my name: 'Master'. Then we drank some milk and ate corn cakes. Friday smiled and enjoyed this food and drink.

We look at the beach

On the next morning we walked to my house. We went past the place of the dead cannibals. Friday wanted to eat them. But I was very angry and took him away from the dead men. We went to the top of the hill and looked at the beach. There were no boats near the beach. The cannibals weren't on my island now, but there were bones on the beach from their dinner. I saw bones from people's heads, arms, hands, legs and feet. So there were other prisoners in the boats.

We made a fire and put the bones on it. Friday was a cannibal, too. He wanted to eat this meat, but I stopped him. He wasn't a cannibal now. He learned this lesson quickly because he was afraid of my gun.

Chapter 10   Friday Changes my Life

Friday in my home

Then we went to my house near the beach. I gave Friday some trousers from the ship, and a coat and hat. They were his first clothes, and he liked them very much. He moved strangely in the clothes, but after some days he was happy with them.

On the next day I thought about a bedroom for Friday. I made a tent for him inside my wall. Then I made a door to my cave at the back. I put my bed in the cave, and at night I slept there. I took my guns and knives into the cave with me, and I shut the door.

But I had no problems with Friday. He was a kind and good friend. He loved me, and he never hurt me in any way. I was very happy with him in my house. He was my child and I taught him about many things.

Friday was afraid of my guns. He talked to them, but he was very careful with them. He never stood near them. I asked him about his conversations with the guns. He said, 'I say, "Please do not kill me." '

My best year

Friday learned everything very quickly. He helped me in many ways. He caught animals and fish and worked in the garden. He cooked for me. He was always happy.

Friday learned English quickly, too. He understood the names for everything, and he began to talk easily in my language. Our conversations were very exciting for me. Friday told me about his life, his family and his island. I listened to his stories and I liked them. These were the best days for me on the island.

Friday's country

One day I asked Friday about his country: 'Does your country

Friday learned everything very quickly.

fight with other countries?'

'Oh, yes,' Friday said. 'We fight and we win.'

'So why were you a prisoner on my beach?'

'There were many of those people. Not many of my people. Those people had good boats. My people do not have strong boats.'

'Friday, what do your people do with their prisoners?' I asked.

'We carry them away. We eat them.'

'Where do you carry them? To this island?'

'Yes, here and other islands.'

'How many people did you eat?' I asked.

'One time we ate twenty men, two women and one child,' he told me.

Then I asked Friday more about his island. This conversation was important for me.

'How near is your home?' I asked.

'It is near. We come here in small boats.'

'And is it dangerous? Do you lose boats when you come here?'

'No,' my slave said, 'the journey is easy.'

I asked Friday many more questions about his home, about the people, the weather, the coasts and beaches. His island was, I understood, in the Caribbean. There were men with white faces to the north. I could go there in a big boat. I wanted to go there one day.

When Friday's English was better, he asked me questions about my country. I told him about England and about other places in Europe. I told him about my family in York and about my sea journeys. A big ship with white men came to his island too, he said. Many men died in the sea, but seventeen people now lived on his island.

'For how many years?' I asked.

'Four years,' said Friday.

'Why don't you eat them?' I asked.

'They are friends. We do not eat friends,' said Friday.

Friday and I make plans

Years later, Friday and I were busy one morning in the garden.

I asked him, 'Friday, do you want to see your country one day?'

'Oh, yes,' he answered.

'What will you do there?'

'I will tell my people about corn bread and dry fruit, about goat meat and books. I will tell them about you, Master. You are kind and good. You helped me.'

'Friday, we can make a boat. You can go to your home,' I told him.

'Why are you angry with me?' asked Friday.

'I am not angry with you,' I answered.

'Why are you sending me away?'

'Don't you want to be at home?' I asked.

'Yes, but with Master,' Friday answered.

'But why?'

'Friday loves Master. Master can teach my people many things. You will come with me in the boat.'

My plan was different from Friday's. I wanted to go to his island. I wanted to see the seventeen white men there. But then I wanted to go to my home – to England – with them.

The idea of a bigger boat was exciting to me and to Friday. We started our work that day and we worked happily for months. The boat was ready in the twenty-seventh year of my time on the island. Now I had a new idea in my head: perhaps this was my last year in this strange land.

But we didn't forget our other jobs. We worked in the garden and we looked after the animals. We made our food. We discussed our journey, and we waited for December. It was the best month for our journey to Friday's country.

Chapter 11   New People

We fight the cannibals

The rain stopped at the end of October. We thought about our journey. One morning Friday went to the beach for some fish. After ten minutes, he ran back to the house. He shouted, 'Master! Master! Oh, bad! Bad!'

'Friday, speak slowly. What happened?'

'Oh, Master! At the beach. Four, five, six boats! Bad men! They eat men!'

'Friday, we can fight them.' I said. 'We have guns. Can you fight, Friday?'

'Yes, Master. I can fight and I can die,' said Friday.

I gave two guns to Friday and I took four other guns. We also had knives with us. Then we went to the top of a hill and looked down at the beach. There were twenty cannibals, three prisoners and three boats. The cannibals stood round a large fire. They cooked and ate the meat from one of their prisoners. The next prisoner for the fire was a white man. He sat on the ground next to a tree.

There were other trees near this prisoner. I ran quietly to those trees and I watched the cannibals. They ate their dinner, and then they wanted more meat. I turned to Friday and said, 'Now, Friday, we have to help this man.'

'I am ready, Master,' he answered.

Very quickly we killed four cannibals with our guns. The other men round the fire jumped up and ran for their boats. They didn't understand the guns, so they were afraid of us. We shouted at them and ran at them with our guns. We killed five more cannibals in their boats. Then I ran to the prisoner and helped him.

A Spanish prisoner

'What is your name?' I asked in Portuguese.

'Christianus,' he answered in Spanish. But he was very weak and couldn't speak very much. I gave him some water and bread. Then I gave him a gun and he stood up. We fought with Friday and we killed more cannibals. Five men left our island in a boat. The other sixteen men were dead.

Friday finds his father

Friday wanted to follow the cannibals and kill them. We ran to a boat and I jumped into it. But inside the boat I found another prisoner. When this man saw me, he was afraid of me. I tried to help him, but he couldn't stand. He was very weak.

Then Friday came to the boat. I said, 'Speak to this prisoner in your language. We are his friends. We have food and drink for him. Tell him that.'

Friday looked at the man's face and he smiled. Then he laughed and jumped up and down. He danced and sang. He hit me on the back. After a time, he was quiet again.

'Speak to me, Friday. Who is this man?' I asked.

'This is my father. I am the happiest son in the world!'

These exciting words stopped me and Christianus. We forgot about the cannibals. Then their boat left the coast, and in minutes we couldn't see it. Then, half an hour later, there was a bad storm. The wind and rain were very strong. Perhaps the cannibals died at sea.

We took the bread and dry fruit from our bags and gave this food to Friday's father. Then Friday ran back to the house and got water and cake for the older man. The water was very good for him. Friday put the Spaniard, Christianus, in the boat next to his father. He ate and drank too. The two men began to feel better. We took them down the coast in the boat and helped them to our house. We put them in our beds, and they slept for hours.

Four people on the island

Now there were four people on the island. Friday and I worked very hard and cooked for our new friends. They enjoyed the corn bread, goat meat, dry fruit and milk. They were strong again after some days in our house. Now they began to talk to us with Friday's help. I didn't know many Spanish words, but Christianus could speak Friday's language. Friday told me his words and his father's words in English.

'Will the cannibals come back to our island?' I asked Friday's father.

'No,' he said in his language. 'They died in the storm, or they are at home. They will not come back here. They do not understand guns. They are afraid of you now, and they will tell their people about the fire from the guns. This fire is fast and strong. It kills everybody and everything. This island is dangerous for them.'

Plans for the future

We forgot about the cannibals and thought about the future. Friday's father said, 'You are a good man. You helped my son and me. My people will help you with a boat. Then you can go to England again.'

I also talked to Christianus about my plan. He said, 'There are sixteen white men on Friday's island. It is not dangerous for them on this island, but they have problems with food and clothes. They do not have anything from their ship. No guns and no tools. Their life is very difficult.'

'What will happen to them?' I asked.

'I do not know. They are very unhappy, but they do not have a boat. They cannot leave the island,' said Christianus.

I thought about this problem for a long time. Then I spoke to Christianus again. 'I have a plan. I want to go to Spanish America. Your men can help me and then they can make the journey with me. Can we bring them here in my boat?'

'Yes, it is a good boat. But what will we do then?' asked Christianus.

'Then we will use my tools and build a small ship. We have food and meat here for a long journey. But I am the master on this island. Will they listen to my words? Will they follow me?' This question was important to me.

'Master Robin, their life is very, very bad. They will fall at your feet and work very hard for you. They want a new life. They are good men. Give them a new life and they will die for you.' This was Christianus's answer to me.

We worked for six months. We put bags of fruit and corn in my cave. We made bread and cakes. We put more fruit in the sun. We made everything ready for sixteen more men on the island and then for a sea journey. This was happy work. We talked and laughed through each day.

At the end of these months, Christianus and Friday's father went back to Friday's island in a small boat. 'Bring your men here as quickly as possible,' I told the Spaniard. 'Then we will build a ship and make our plans.'

They left with a good wind behind them in the month of October. After twenty-seven years and some days on this island, I hoped for a good future.

Chapter 12   Men on the Island

A ship

After eight days without Friday's father and Christianus, Friday ran into my tent and shouted, 'Master, Master, they are here! They are here!'

I jumped out of my bed and pulled on my clothes. I didn't think. I didn't take my gun. I ran to the beach with Friday. We looked at the sea and saw a boat about four miles from the coast. The wind brought the boat nearer to us at the south end of the island.

I said, 'These are not the people from your island.'

'Who are they?' asked Friday. 'Are they friends, too?'

'I don't know. We have to go to the top of the hill and look at them.'

When we were on the hill, we saw the boat and also a large ship.

After twenty-seven years and some days on this island,
I hoped for a good future.

The ship was about seven miles from our coast. It was an English ship! I felt very excited. Was this possible? Were these Englishmen and friends? But why were they here? The English didn't have land in these places. The weather was good, so there were no problems with storms in these months. I had to watch and wait.

Englishmen on the beach

The boat was on the beach in a short time. The men were about half a mile away from Friday and me. There were eleven men, but two stayed in the boat. Six men left the boat with guns in their hands. The other three men were prisoners. The men with guns pushed the prisoners out of the boat and on to the beach. What did this mean?

Friday said, 'You see, Master. Englishmen eat other men, too.'

'No,' I said. 'They will not eat their prisoners. Perhaps they will kill them, but they will not eat them.'

The men with guns looked up and down the beach. The three prisoners sat down. They were very sad. They knew nothing about their future. They were afraid of the men with guns.

The two men in the boat shouted to the other men because the sea was not as high as before. Now they couldn't move the boat for some hours. These two men left the boat, too, and walked with the other men with guns.

The three prisoners' story

Friday and I watched. Our guns were ready for a fight. We waited for the night. But at two o'clock in the afternoon, when it was very hot, the men went to sleep under some trees. The three prisoners didn't sleep. I wanted to speak to them. I wanted to know their story. I came near them very quietly and said, 'Who are you, good men?'

The prisoners jumped. Their eyes were very big and they couldn't speak.

'Do not be afraid. Perhaps I can be your friend,' I told them.

'Nobody can help us, sir. We are dead men,' answered one prisoner.

'You are wrong. I am an Englishman and I can help you. Tell me your story. What happened to you?'

'Our story, sir, is very sad,' said the oldest prisoner. 'I was the captain of that ship. There were some bad men on the ship. They had guns, and they made me a prisoner. They took the ship away from me. Now they will kill us or leave us in this place. They are bad men. They will kill you, too.'

'There are eight men under those trees. Are they all bad?' I asked.

'No, sir, many of them are good men, but there are two very bad men. They are the new masters.'

Robinson Crusoe helps the Englishmen

'Come with me,' I told the prisoners. 'We will make a plan. But first, listen to me. I am the master on this island. You have to listen to me.'

'Sir, you are very kind and good. We will listen and follow you. Our ship, too, is yours. We will take it back to England with you and your man Friday in it,' said the captain.

'Good. But first, our plan for today.' I gave each prisoner a gun and we walked back to the beach. The other men were asleep, but our noise woke them up. The captain and his two men killed the two worst men. The other six men were now the captain's prisoners.

I sat down in my house with the captain. He asked me about my story and I told him about my twenty-seven years on this island. We talked about my problems and about my house, my garden, my animals and my man Friday. Then I gave him and his two men very good food and drink. I showed them my things. They listened happily to the story of my life.

Chapter 13   The End of the Fight

Another boat comes from the ship

The next morning the captain and I sat down and talked about the ship. Friday took our six prisoners to the big cave near my country house. He left them there.

'How many men are on the ship now?' I asked the captain.

'Twenty-six,' he answered.

'What will they do?'

'I think that they will send a boat to the island. They will look for the other men,' said the captain.

'We have to move your boat. Then, when the men come from the ship, they will not see it. They will have to look for the other men. Then we can stop them with our guns. You will be captain of the ship again.'

'That is a good plan,' said the captain.

That afternoon a boat with ten men left the ship and came to the beach. Each man carried a gun. We watched these men from the top of the hill. The captain looked at them. Three or four were good men. Two were very dangerous.

I smiled at the captain. 'Do not be afraid. We are ready and they do not know about us. We will win this fight.'

The men stay on the island

On the beach, the men from the ship shouted for their friends. Then they used their guns and made a lot of noise. There was no answer. After some time they sat on the beach and talked. It was very hot again, but these men didn't go to sleep. We watched and waited.

Then the ten men walked down the beach to their boat. Were they on their way to the ship? They had to stay on the island. I thought quickly.

'Run behind the trees!' I told Friday and the captain's man.

Then they shouted very loudly and made a lot of noise.

We take more prisoners

The ten men looked round quickly. Then eight men ran to the sound from the trees. When they were near, Friday and the other man moved away and shouted again. The men from the ship followed this sound for hours.

When the eight men left the beach, the captain and his other men ran to the boat.

'Stop or you will die,' shouted the captain. 'You are now our prisoners.'

The two men put their guns on the ground.

It was late and very dark when the other eight men from the ship came back to the beach. They were now weak and tired.

'There is nobody in our boat!' shouted one of the men.

'What happened? Where are our friends?' somebody asked.

'This is a very strange island. I don't like it here,' another man said.

They called their friends' names. Nobody answered.

Very quietly we came nearer them. But the captain couldn't wait. He killed the worst man with his gun and hit another man. That man died two hours later. Then we all ran at them, and the captain shouted, 'Tom Smith, Tom Smith!'

Tom Smith answered, 'Who's that? Captain? Is it you?'

'Yes, Tom Smith. I am your captain. Throw down your guns. We are very strong.'

The men put down their guns. Now we had six new prisoners.

The captain goes back to his ship

The next morning we went to the big cave and looked at our fourteen prisoners. The captain said, 'You will all die in England. You took the ship from me. You were wrong.'

The prisoners cried and asked the captain for their lives. He talked to each prisoner. Some men were good and some men were bad. In the end, the captain took nine good men back to his ship. He left the other five men on the island.

At midnight the captain took his men and his two boats and went back to his ship. There they killed the new 'captain' and his friends with their guns. Then they made a loud noise with the ship's big guns. The ship was theirs again.

Chapter 14   I Go Home

My last day on my island

On the island, we heard the captain's guns and we slept well. When I woke up the next morning, the captain stood next to my bed.

'Master Crusoe, our great friend, wake up. Look! Your ship

is ready. It is yours, and we are your slaves,' said the captain very kindly.

I looked out to sea. The ship was about half a mile from the beach. I couldn't speak for some minutes. I nearly fell to the ground. Then I cried, because I was very happy. The captain put his arms round me, and then I was quiet.

The captain gave me food and drink from the ship. We ate and talked about the journey. Then he gave me some wonderful clothes: shoes, trousers, shirt, jacket and a hat. And everything was new!

I say goodbye

Before we left the island, the captain and I talked to the five prisoners. They had to stay on the island. I told them about my house and garden and about the animals. They had many things for their new life. I told them about Christianus, the Spaniard, and Friday's father – good men and good friends. I wrote a letter and left it for Christianus. I told him about the prisoners and about Friday.

I carried some things with me to the ship. I took my hat, my umbrella and my parrot. I forgot to take the money. I left it under my bed. And so, with my man Friday, I left the island on 19th December in the year 1686.

Chapter 15   A New Life

I am a rich man

When I came to England again, it was 11th June in the year 1687. I put my foot on English land for the first time in thirty-five years. I had no money, but the ship's captain didn't forget me. His bosses gave me two hundred pounds because I helped the captain on my island.

I went to the north of the country and visited York. Everything was very different. My father and mother were dead, but I found two sisters and the two children of my older brother. They didn't have much money, and I wanted to help them.

I made a new plan. My man Friday and I went to Lisbon in Portugal. We wanted to speak to somebody about my farm in Brazil. The money from my farm came to a bank in Lisbon each year. I had about five thousand pounds in the bank, so I stayed in Lisbon for seven months. Then I sold the farm. I had twenty thousand pounds. Now I was a rich man.

I help my family

I went to York again and I helped my sisters and my brother's children. I sent the children to school. After some years, I put the older boy on a farm. I sent the younger boy to sea with a good captain.

And I found a wife. We lived in London, and we had three children: two sons and a daughter. I was happy with my new family, but then my wife died. My brother's younger son talked to me about the sea again.

I see my island again

In 1694, Friday and I went back to my island. There were a lot of men and women there now. We visited them and listened to their story. The Spaniards, with Christianus and Friday's father, came back to the island after we left. They lived and worked with the

English prisoners. Then more men and some women came from Spanish America. Now there were twenty children on the island, too. We stayed with them for three weeks and gave them many things from our ship.

We also visited Brazil. I sent more people and animals to my island from there. Perhaps I will live on my island again in the future. But that will be a different story.

ACTIVITIES

Chapters 1–5

Before you read

1 Do you know the name Robinson Crusoe? What do you know about this man?

2 Find these words in your dictionary. They are all in the story.

cannibal cave coast corn farm goat hill island land mark parrot slave storm tent tool umbrella

   a Which words are for people?
   b Which are for animals and birds?
   c What can people live in?
   d Where do horses and chickens live?
   e What do they eat?
   f Which can you find on a good map?
   g What do you carry when it rains?
   h What can you use when you build a house?
   i Which is a word for bad weather?
   j What does dirty water leave on a white wall?

After you read

3 Are these sentences about Robinson Crusoe right or wrong?
   a He always listens to his father.
   b He visits two countries outside England before 1659.
   c He finds a good house on the island.
   d He moves his house away from the beach.
   e He eats a lot of dry fruit in September.
   f He doesn't like cannibals.
   g He is happier at the end of his second year on the island.
   h He has an old umbrella from the ship.
   i He teaches his parrot English words.

Chapters 6–10

Before you read

4 Do you think that Robinson's life is exciting? Why (not)?

5 Find these words in your dictionary:

bone master prisoner

Which word goes with these words?

a boss clever follow important top

b catch dangerous detective gun police station

c white arm leg back break

After you read

6 How does Robinson Crusoe's life change after he sees:

a the mark of a foot on the beach?

b bones on the beach?

c cannibals on the beach?

d Friday?

Chapters 11–15

Before you read

7 Do you think that Robinson Crusoe will leave the island? How?

8 What can a *captain* be the boss of? Look in your dictionary.

After you read

9 Which of the people in the story:

a can speak English and a language from an island?

b is from Spain?

c leave bones on the beach?

d makes Friday very happy?

e helps his family in York?

f gives Robinson Crusoe some fine clothes?

10 Work with another student. Have this conversation.

Student A: You are Robinson Crusoe. You are in England, but you are going to go back to your island. Tell Friday.

Student B: You are Friday. Listen to Robinson Crusoe. What do you think? Tell him. Then ask questions.

Writing

11 You are Robinson Crusoe. Write about a day on the island when nothing important happens.

12 You are the captain of the English ship at the end of the book. Write your story for a newspaper.

13 You are Robinson Crusoe. You are in England after thirty-five years, and you are going to go to York. Write a letter to your sister. Say that you are not dead. You will see her in two or three days.

14 Would you like to be Robinson Crusoe? Why (not)?

Answers for the Activities in this book are available from your local Pearson Education office or: Penguin Readers Marketing Department, Pearson Education, Edinburgh Gate, Harlow, Essex, CM20 2JE.